ECOCRAFTS

Gorgeous Gifts

ECOCRAFTS

Gorgeous
Gifts

KINGFISHER
BOSTON

KINGFISHER

a Houghton Mifflin Company imprint
222 Berkeley Street
Boston, Massachusetts 02116
www.houghtonmifflinbooks.com

First published in 2007
2 4 6 8 10 9 7 5 3 1

1TR/0107/C&C/MAR(MAR)/128OJIEX-GREEN/C

Author: Rebecca Craig

For Toucan
Editor: Theresa Bebbington
Design: Leah Germann
Additional craft makers: Dawn Brend,
Melanie Williams, Kirsty Neale
Photography art direction: Jane Thomas
Editorial assistant: Hannah Bowen
Photographer: Andy Crawford
Editorial director: Ellen Dupont

For Kingfisher
Editorial manager: Russell Mclean
Coordinating editor: Caitlin Doyle
Art director: Mike Davis
Senior production controller: Lindsey Scott
DTP coordinator: Catherine Hibbert
DTP operator: Claire Cessford

LIBRARY OF CONGRESS CATALOGING-IN-PUBLICATION DATA
Craig, Rebecca, 1983–
Ecocrafts: Gorgeous gifts/Rebecca Craig.—1st ed.
p. cm.
Includes index.
1. Handicraft—Juvenile literature.
2. Recycling (Waste, etc.)—Juvenile literature.
3. Gifts—Juvenile literature. I. Title
TT160.C784 2007
745.5—dc22
2006024810

ISBN 978-0-7534-5967-6

Printed in China

**The paper used for the cover and inside pages
is made from 100% recycled post-consumer waste.**

Contents

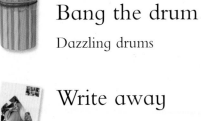

Ecowise

When you give a gift that you have made yourself, you are giving a special present. It's a one of a kind. There won't be another one just like it anywhere in the world! And the person you give it to will love it because you took the time to make it for them.

3 Rs to recycling

Around half of our garbage can be recycled. Follow these steps to help prevent garbage from being sent to landfills or incinerators.

REDUCE—Encourage your parents to buy products that have little or no packaging.

REUSE—Find new ways to use jars, cans, plastic containers, and other durable items.

RECYCLE—If you can't reuse something but it can be recycled, help your parents recycle it.

As well as being really special, all of the projects in this book help the environment by using everyday objects found in your home. A lot of them are things that you would have thrown away. Inside you'll find ways to use an old sweater and some cardboard to make a mousepad, newspaper and magazines to make a colorful bracelet, and even an old potato chip bag to make a gift bag. Recycling helps the planet because it reuses things that would have ended up in the trash.

Around the world, tons of garbage end up in landfills each year. In fact, in 1999 the Fresh

Kills landfill in Staten Island, New York, became the largest human-made structure in the world, overtaking the Great Wall of China. Because air and water cannot reach the garbage buried deep in the landfill, the garbage doesn't decompose, or break down. Even after 30 years you can still read newspapers buried in a landfill!

Sometimes garbage goes to an incinerator, where it is burned. But this isn't a good solution either. The ashes still have to be disposed of—and they can be toxic (poisonous). Burning garbage also creates air pollution. The only really good way to reduce waste is to recycle. For example, by recycling plastic, 50 percent less energy is used than if it was burned in an incinerator. And the plastic can be used to make something else—such as a fleece jacket or even a park bench.

What you can do

Unwrap a present carefully so that you can reuse the wrapping paper. Save the bows and ribbons to wrap another gift.

Cut up some cardboard to make gift tags and then decorate them.

Use your old drawings, paintings, and other artwork as wrapping paper. You can also reuse old newspapers or maps as wrapping paper.

Save cardboard boxes from your toys, shoes, or even candy. You can reuse them by putting gifts in them and then decorating or wrapping the boxes.

When buying a gift, buy one that is more durable. It can last longer than several cheaper versions, so fewer items will end up in a landfill.

Getting started

Before starting a project, make sure that you have everything you need. If you don't know how to trace a picture or make papier-mâché, follow the steps here. Some craft supplies are not supposed to be used by children under 13. If you're not sure if something is safe to use, ask an adult if it's okay. When using craft supplies that have a strong odor, work in a room that has plenty of fresh air. If an object is difficult to cut, ask an adult to help.

ruler

scissors

pen

pencil

paintbrush

tape

paint

glue

TRACING A PICTURE

If you have a pencil, pen, tracing paper, and tape, you can copy any picture you want. The pencil should have soft lead (No. 2)—this will make it easier to do the rubbing over the back. Use a pen with a hard point to make the lines really sharp.

STEP 1
Tape down a sheet of tracing paper over the picture that you want to draw. Using a pen with a hard point, trace the picture onto the tracing paper.

STEP 2
Remove the tracing paper from the picture. Rub a pencil on the back of the tracing paper where you can see the lines that you have drawn.

STEP 3
Tape the paper onto the object where you want the picture to be. Draw over the lines in pen. Remove the tracing paper. The design will be on the object.

MAKING PAPIER-MÂCHÉ

By soaking newspaper in a paste made from flour and water, you can mold and build up many shapes. Use long strips of newspaper when you need to add strength.

Smaller pieces of newspaper are easier for molding. Build up layers until you have the shape that you want. Let the paper dry completely before decorating it.

STEP 1

Measure out one part flour to around two parts water. For example, use one cup of flour and two cups of water. Mix four tablespoons of salt with the flour to prevent the papier-mâché from getting moldy.

STEP 2

Pour the water over the flour. Mix with a wooden spoon until you have a smooth paste without lumps— it should look like thick glue. If it is too thick, add a little more water. If it is too thin, add some more flour.

STEP 3

Rip up some newspaper into strips, following the steps for your project. Dip a strip of newspaper into the paste until it is really soaked. It is now ready to use.

9

Starry jars

You can transform an old jar into a beautiful tea light candleholder. If you want to paint the jar with nail polish, first ask an adult and paint in an airy room.

YOU WILL NEED:

small glass jar, scrubbing brush, cardboard, pen, ruler, scissors, nail polish (or thin, water-based acrylic paint or glass paint), paintbrush, flexible wire (for hanging the candleholder)

STEP 1

Clean out the jar carefully. First let it soak in soapy water to help remove the label and then scrub off the label. Let the jar dry completely.

STEP 2

Cut a long strip of cardboard that is the same height as your jar—but don't include the "neck" of the jar. You can use a pen and a ruler to mark where to cut the cardboard and then cut it with a pair of scissors.

STEP 3

To get the cardboard strip to be the right length, wrap it tightly around the jar. Then draw a line with the pen where the end meets the cardboard. Remove the cardboard and cut along this line with your scissors.

STEP 4

Draw a design on the cardboard strip with a pen. Stars and a moon have been used here but draw anything you want to—you could try animals, flowers, or rocket ships.

STEP 5

Roll up the cardboard with the design facing out. Place it inside of the jar (you'll use it to copy your design onto the jar). Make sure that the cardboard is straight.

STEP 6

Paint your design onto the jar by tracing the design on the cardboard. Let the paint dry and remove the cardboard. Your candleholder is ready for a tea light!

Starry jars

STEP 7

For the hanger:
Ask a grownup to cut a long piece of flexible wire. Twist the ends together to form a loop. Center the wire around the jar's "neck" and then twist tightly at both sides so that the wire is tight around the jar.

STEP 8

Twist the wire together, all the way to the ends, until it is completely twisted— but leave a small loop on one end.

STEP 9

Push the twisted end of the wire into the loop on the other end. Then twist it back around itself to fasten the two ends together.

12

Starry jar tea light candleholders have a pretty glow when the tea lights are lit at night. Ask an adult to help you hang them in a safe place.

Pretty plants

Make a cool plant pot for a relative, teacher, or friend. This is a really fun and easy project and a great way to recycle yogurt cups or other plastic containers.

YOU WILL NEED:
•••

yogurt cup (or other plastic container), paintbrush, glue, string, scissors, paint, ribbon

STEP 1

Turn the container upside down and use a paintbrush to spread an even layer of glue all over the outside.

STEP 2

Start to wind the string around the container, starting at the base. Make sure that the end of the string is firmly tucked under the first two or three wraps. Wind the string tightly, with no gaps.

14

STEP **3**

Continue winding the string around the container until you reach the rim. Using scissors, trim off any extra string and tuck the end neatly under the last few wraps of string to hide it. Let the glue dry completely.

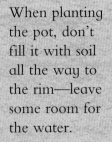

When planting the pot, don't fill it with soil all the way to the rim—leave some room for the water.

STEP **4**

Paint the plant pot any color you want to. If you want a really nice finish, ask an adult to spray-paint the plant pot. When the paint is dry, tie a ribbon around it, making a neat bow.

On your mark

Do you have a brother, sister, or friend who always has his or her nose in a book? A pretty bookmark made from coffee stirrers would make a great gift.

YOU WILL NEED:

coffee stirrers (or disposable chopsticks or Popsicle sticks), colorful string (or ribbon or embroidery thread), scissors, clip

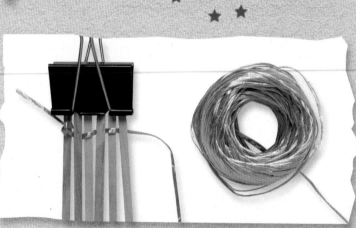

ECOFACT

Unlike plastic stirrers, wooden stirrers come from a renewable source. When the trees that supply the wood are cut down, new trees can be planted. Plastics are made from oil, which will eventually run out.

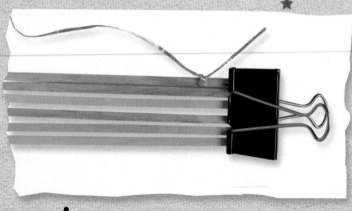

STEP 1

Ask an adult to put five or six coffee stirrers into a clip—this will hold them together firmly while you work. Tie the end of the string to the first stirrer, close to the edge of the clip.

STEP 2

Weave the string under and over each coffee stirrer until you reach the last stirrer.

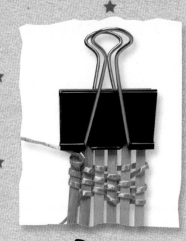

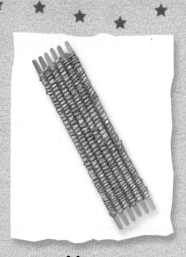

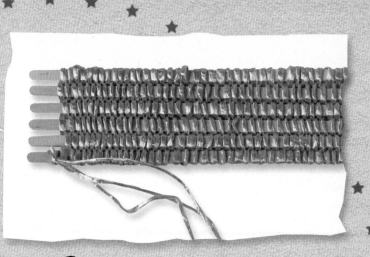

STEP 3

Wrap the string around the last stirrer and then continue weaving in the opposite direction. Make sure that you weave under and over in an opposite pattern from the previous row of weaving.

STEP 4

Continue weaving the rows as you did in Step 3, changing the weaving pattern for each row, until you reach the end of the stirrers.

STEP 5

Knot the end of the string around the last stirrer to hold it in place. You can also make a tassle by adding a few extra pieces of string to the knotted end.

Strings in different colors will make your bookmark stand out.

Beautiful bracelet

This bracelet is entirely made out of scrap paper, but don't worry—once it's dry, the bracelet will be as solid as a rock and ready for you to decorate however you want to.

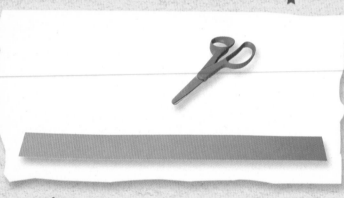

YOU WILL NEED:
....
cardboard, scissors, pencil, ruler, tape, flour and water paste, newspaper, paintbrush, glossy magazines, glue

STEP 1
Cut out a strip of cardboard as wide as you want your bracelet to be and long enough to fit over your hand or the hand of the person who will wear it. You can use a pencil and a ruler to draw straight lines as a cutting guide.

STEP 2
Form a circle with the cardboard strip and tape the ends together. The circle should be a little bit too large so that there's room for the papier-mâché.

STEP 3
Mix together a flour and water paste (see pages 8–9). Tear some newspapers into long strips, around the width of your finger. To make the bracelet strong, tear wider chunks too.

18

STEP 4

Cover the strips with paste and wind them around the bracelet. Make sure that the newspaper is smooth, with no bumps, and well covered in paste.

STEP 5

To make your bracelet chunky, scrunch a sheet of newspaper into a thick strip and paste it around the outside of the bracelet.

STEP 6

Cover the outer chunk with smaller strips of newspaper until it is smooth. Let the bracelet dry overnight. Once it is dry, it will be hard and firm.

STEP 7

Dip some strips cut out from a magazine in glue and wrap them around the bracelet. Once the glue is dry, your bracelet is ready to wear.

For a really shiny finish, ask a grownup to cover your bracelet with a coat of varnish.

You can decorate your bracelets by painting them or by adding pictures from magazines such as these flowers or butterfly shapes.

Sock-puppy puppets

Why not recycle your old socks and turn them into a great gift for a younger brother or sister. With a little imagination, your old socks can become anything you want them to be. Will your puppet have teeth? Eyebrows? Whiskers? A mustache?

YOU WILL NEED:

old sock, pen, scissors, scraps of fabric and/or felt, glue, rubber bands, three buttons, needle and thread, paint, paintbrush

STEP 1

Lie the sock out flat, make a line on the sock halfway down the toes with a pen and then cut along the line with scissors. Repeat on the other side so that there are two slits.

STEP 2

Put the sock over your hand. To make the mouth, push the end of the sock inside, until all the fabric up to the end of the slits closest to the heel is inside of the sock. The slits will make the mouth less bulky.

STEP 3

Draw an oval shape onto the fabric. Make sure that it will be large enough to fit over the puppet's mouth. Cut out the oval shape.

STEP 4

Spread some glue on one side of the oval-shaped fabric. Place the oval over the mouth, with the glued side facing the sock. Make sure that the slits are not peeping out from behind the oval.

STEP 5

To make the dog's ears, fold a piece of fabric or felt in half. Cut a long, thin oval in the fabric—these will make two identical ears.

Sock-puppy puppets

STEP 6

Glue the ears onto each side of the heel of the sock. Let the glue dry. (To make them really secure, ask an adult to sew them once the glue has dried.)

STEP 7

Cut out a shaggy shape from the fabric or felt to make the dog's eye patch. Make it any shape you want. Glue the patch where you will be placing an eye (see Step 10).

STEP 8

Cut out a piece of red fabric to make the tongue. Glue it inside of the mouth. (Again, you can ask an adult to sew the tongue to make it secure once the glue has dried.)

STEP 9

For a great finishing touch, cut a pair of rubber bands so that they no longer form loops and then thread them through a large button to make a nose with whiskers.

STEP 10

Ask an adult to sew on a pair of buttons as eyes and a larger button as a nose. Dab a blob of black paint onto the lighter colored buttons to really make the eyes stand out.

Turn the page to learn how to make this fun puppet theater!

Although we've made a puppy, you can follow these steps to create all types of exciting puppet animals such as a fierce dragon or a cute kitten.

Curtains up!

You can transform a large cardboard box into a fantastic puppet theater—a perfect place to show off a pair of cool sock-puppy puppets (turn to page 20 to make this project).

YOU WILL NEED:
cardboard box, glue, ruler, pencil, scissors, paint, paintbrush, thick cardboard, black fabric, white chalk, velvet fabric, gold cord, small knitting needle

STEP 1

If your box has any open sides, glue them closed. Then, use a ruler and a pencil to draw a narrow border around one large side. Cut out the area inside of your pencil lines.

STEP 2

Draw two circles onto the back of the box, close to the bottom. Cut them out and then check that the holes that are left behind are big enough to comfortably fit your hand (and puppet) through.

24

STEP 3

Paint the inside of your box black. Once it is dry, add another coat and let that dry. Then paint a dark color along the top, back, and sides of the box and the bottom edge of the "frame." Let it dry and then add a bright paint to the top and the side edges of the "frame."

STEP 4

Trace the shape of the top of your box onto thick cardboard. Using this as a guide, draw a curvy pediment around it—it will sit above your theater stage. Cut out the pediment.

STEP 5

In pencil, draw stripes that curve out from the top to the bottom. The direction of the curve will change in the middle of the pediment.

STEP 6

Using a paintbrush, paint every other stripe with a bright color such as yellow. Then paint the remaining stripes in a contrasting bright color.

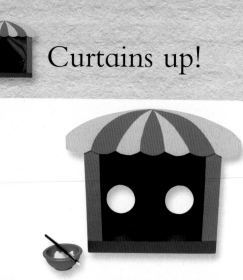

Curtains up!

STEP 7

Brush a lot of glue along the top edge of the "frame" on your box. Carefully press the pediment on top of it, making sure that it's centered. Lie the box on its back while the glue dries so that the pediment does not fall off.

STEP 8

Trace around the back of your box onto a piece of black fabric. A piece of white chalk will be easy to see. Cut out the fabric and brush glue along all four edges. Allow it to dry. This stops the fabric from fraying.

STEP 9

Spread glue along one long edge of the fabric on the side that you will not see. Press it along the top of the back wall, inside of the box. Lie the box flat until the glue is dry.

STEP 10

Trace around the back of the box onto the back of some velvet. Make the bottom edge 2 in. (5cm) longer and then cut it out. Fold the fabric in half and cut along the fold. Seal the edges with glue and allow it to dry.

26

STEP 11

Add glue to the narrow edge of one piece, on the velvety side of the fabric. Press it into place behind the pediment, inside of your box. Add the second curtain in the same way. Let the glue dry.

STEP 12

With a small knitting needle, make two small holes in one side of your box, close to the front and around halfway up. They should be around 0.5 in. (1.5cm) apart. Cut 10 in. (25cm) of gold cord and poke the ends through the holes. Repeat on the other side of the box.

STEP 13

Pull a curtain to each side and use the cord to tie them in place.

If you can't find red velvet, purple or green will make dramatic curtains too.

Hanging a black cloth on the back of your stage will cover the holes when you are not using them. When you put your puppet through the hole, the material will bunch up around your arm.

27

Bang the drum

A strong, round, empty container will make a great drum for any budding musician in the family. Make sure that your container is empty and clean before you start the project!

YOU WILL NEED:
• •
large, round container, paint, paintbrushes, pencil, small ruler, greaseproof paper, small bowl or saucer, glue, tissue paper, colored rubber (or hair) bands

STEP 1

Paint your container white all over and allow it to dry. You don't have to worry about making this layer of paint too neat—it's just to help with the next stage.

30

STEP 2

Using a small ruler and a pencil, draw vertical stripes on the white background. You can make them all different widths, or, if you prefer, the same size.

STEP 3

Paint every other stripe, alternating between colors of your choice. Bright colors will stand out more.

STEP 4

When the painted stripes are completely dry, fill in the stripes between them with two more paint colors. Allow these to dry too.

STEP 5

For the skin of the drum, use a bowl that is a couple of inches wider than your drum and put it on some greaseproof paper. Trace around it. Cut out the circle.

Bang the drum

STEP 6

Spread glue all over one side of the circle. Use a lot of glue and spread it out smoothly. This will make the drum skin tight.

STEP 7

While the glue is wet, stretch the greaseproof paper over the top of the drum as tightly as you can, with the extra paper folded down the sides of the drum.

STEP 8

Cut out a circle from some colorful tissue paper, just like you did from the greaseproof paper. Brush glue all over one side and smooth it over the paper on top of your drum.

STEP 9

To hold the greaseproof paper and tissue paper in place as they dry, and to add some extra decoration, carefully stretch one or two colored rubber bands around the sides of the drum. Or try using stretched-out hair bands.

32

You can paint your drums any pattern that you like. Or cut out shapes, such as stars, circles, or flowers, from colorful wrapping paper and glue these onto the drum.

Make a whole set of drums by using containers of different sizes.

Write away

Is there someone in your family who loves writing letters? Surprise them with their own personalized stationery set made from discarded envelopes and magazines. It's a cool way to recycle!

YOU WILL NEED:

envelope from a holiday or birthday card, tracing paper, pencil, scissors, cardboard, tape, pen, large envelopes, glue stick, magazine pictures

ECOFACT

The number one material to be thrown away is paper. office paper can be recycled into newsprint, paper for books and magazines, and stationery. Recycling paper uses less chemicals and bleaches than making paper from trees.

STEP 1

Carefully take apart an old envelope and use it to make a template. Trace around the envelope and its folds onto tracing paper (see pages 8–9). Transfer it onto cardboard.

STEP 2

Cut out the template, being careful around any little indentations on the corners. Put the template over a large piece of magazine paper, draw around it, and cut along the lines.

34

STEP 3

Fold in the bottom flap. Now fold in the two side flaps and stick them to the bottom flap using a glue stick.

STEP 4

Now make the writing paper. On the back of a large used envelope, use a pencil and a ruler to draw a rectangle that will be large enough for writing a letter.

STEP 5

Use a pair of scissors to cut the paper along the rectangle. Try to keep the lines as straight as you can.

STEP 6

To decorate the writing paper, cut out pictures from a magazine. Cut them into small squares or other shapes. Glue them onto the paper—make sure that you leave space for writing!

High flier

You can use a take-away container to make a flying airplane that will zoom around your room! Make sure that you clean the container and let it dry first.

YOU WILL NEED:

tracing paper, pencil, scissors, cardboard, ruler, Styrofoam container, felt-tip pen, paint, paintbrush, paper clip

ECOFACT

Styrofoam, used to make take-away food containers, cannot be recycled. This plastic often drifts into drains and sewers. It then flows into the sea and breaks up into tiny pieces. It can be eaten by marine life, which may die from it.

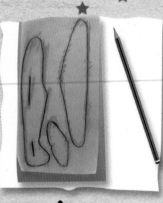

STEP 1

Trace the templates for the airplane (see pages 46–47), using a pencil and tracing paper to transfer them onto cardboard (see pages 8–9).

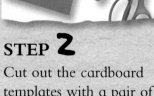

STEP 2

Cut out the cardboard templates with a pair of scissors, cutting carefully to keep the lines straight.

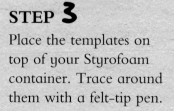

STEP 3

Place the templates on top of your Styrofoam container. Trace around them with a felt-tip pen.

STEP 4

Carefully cut out the three airplane shapes from the Styrofoam using a pair of sharp scissors.

STEP 5

Ask an adult to use a craft knife to cut two slits in the body of the airplane, just wide enough for the wings to fit in.

STEP 6

Paint any pattern you want on the pieces of the airplane. Let the paint dry on one side before painting the other side.

STEP 7

To assemble the airplane, push the small wings into the slit at the back of the body and the big wings into the slit at the front.

STEP 8

Push a paper clip onto the nose of the plane. This will add weight to the front of the plane, which will help it fly.

Then paint a cockpit for the pilot—choose any colors you want.

Your airplane is now ready for a test flight!

Bright lights

You can make an amazing window decoration by cutting silhouette shapes out of two layers of black paper and using colorful candy wrappers to create "stained glass."

YOU WILL NEED:
....

tracing paper, pen, white chalk or grease pencil, black cardboard or paper, scissors, see-through candy wrappers, glue stick or tape, glue, paintbrush

STEP 1

Trace the leaf design (see page 47) onto tracing paper (see page 8).

STEP 2

Rub a white pencil or chalk over the back of the tracing and transfer the stencil onto the black paper.

STEP 3

To cut out a "window pane," gently fold the paper over, making sure that it doesn't crease. Cut into the fold, in an area that will be a pane. Unfold the paper and continue the cut to a line and then cut along the line.

38

STEP 4

Repeat Step 3 until you have cut out all of the window panes.

STEP 5

Turn over the black paper. Cut a candy wrapper so that it fits tightly over a pane and tape or glue it down. Repeat this step for each pane.

STEP 6

If you want a glossy finish, spread glue over your window. Let it dry.

Hang your "stained glass" in a window that gets a lot of light.

We have used a leaf pattern, but you can use other stencils or make your own. Why not try a rabbit, a rocket ship, or stars and a crescent moon?

39

Mighty mouse

Why not make a mousepad for a computer-loving friend or relative? Our mousepad features a cute mouse, but you can draw your own design instead.

YOU WILL NEED:
tracing paper, pencil, strong cardboard (the cardboard from a board-backed envelope is perfect), scissors, paint, paintbrushes, waterproof black felt-tip pen, glue, old woolen sweater or blanket, thin paper, pins

ECoFACT
Even if clothes have become too old to wear and are not suitable for a secondhand store, they can still be used by industrial companies as rags. Sweaters and other items that are made from wool can be respun, and these fibers can be used again.

STEP 1
Trace the mouse template on page 43, including the eyes, ears, nose, mouth, and whiskers (see pages 8–9). Transfer the tracing onto a piece of thick cardboard.

STEP 2
Neatly cut around the outside edges of the cardboard. Make sure that you are careful on the corners around the ears.

STEP 3

Paint the mouse's face and the edges of its ears in a light color. Don't worry about going over the mouth and whiskers—when the paint dries, you will still be able to see faint marks if you press your pencil down.

STEP 4

When the paint is dry, use a small brush to paint the center of the ears in a bright color, the nose in a pale color, and the eyes white. Allow it to dry.

STEP 5

With a black felt-tip pen, carefully outline the eyes and add some pupils. Outline the nose and the center of the ears and then draw on the mouth and the whiskers.

STEP 6

To protect your mousepad and give it a glossy finish, brush on two or three coats of glue. Spread the glue smoothly, but not too thin. Allow each coat to dry before adding the next.

Mighty mouse

STEP 7

Ask an adult to wash your wool item on the hottest cycle in a washing machine. The wool will turn into felt and be smaller when it comes out. It will also feel thicker and won't fray when you cut it. Let the felted wool dry.

STEP 8

Trace the mouse again—this time onto a piece of thin scrap paper—and cut it out.

STEP 9

Pin the paper shape to your felted wool. Cut out around the mouse shape.

STEP 10

Cover the back of your cardboard mouse with glue. Carefully place the felt mouse shape on top and smooth it down. Rest books on top of the mousepad until the glue dries.

The smooth surface makes the mousepad ideal for a computer mouse.

Mousepad template

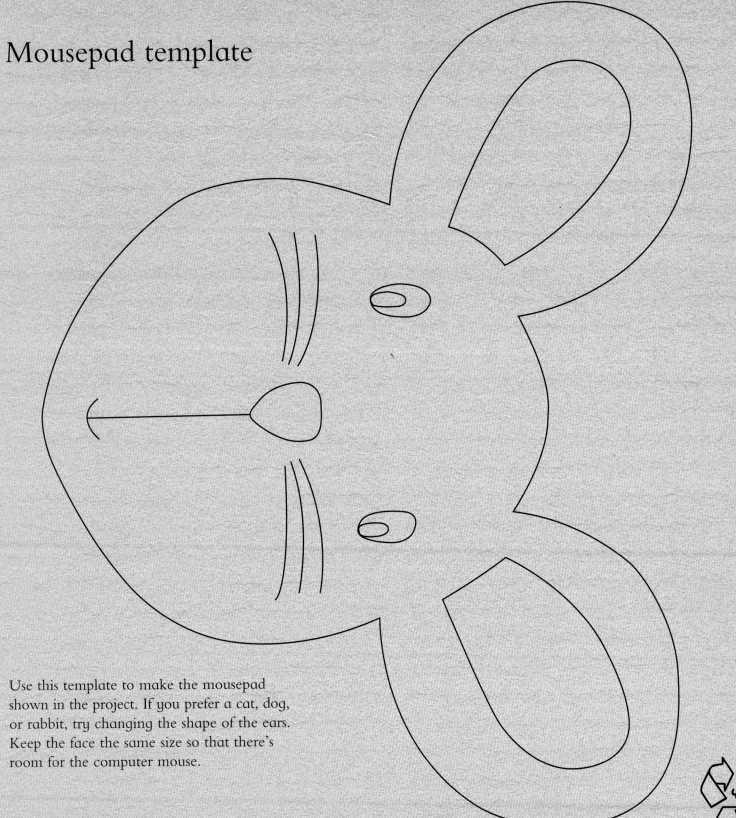

Use this template to make the mousepad
shown in the project. If you prefer a cat, dog,
or rabbit, try changing the shape of the ears.
Keep the face the same size so that there's
room for the computer mouse.

43

It's a wrap!

Now that you've made some great presents, how will you wrap them? Here's a cool way to reuse a potato chip bag for a sturdy gift. (It's not ideal for delicate gifts such as silk scarves!)

YOU WILL NEED:
....

potato chip bag (with shiny foil inside), paper towel, tape, ribbon or string, scissors

STEP 1

Thoroughly wash out a large potato chip bag. Let the bag dry. Turn it inside out by pushing the bottom of the bag through the top half.

STEP 2

Use a paper towel to rub the bag thoroughly to make sure that all traces of food have been removed. If the paper towel becomes dirty or greasy, clean your bag again. Allow the bag to dry.

STEP 3

Turn over around 3 in. (10cm) of the top edge, inside of the bag. Tape it down to create a finished edge.

STEP 4

Place your gift inside of the bag. Cut a piece of ribbon or colored string. Tie it around the bag and make a large, neat bow.

Fluff out the bag above the ribbon to give it a finishing touch.

45

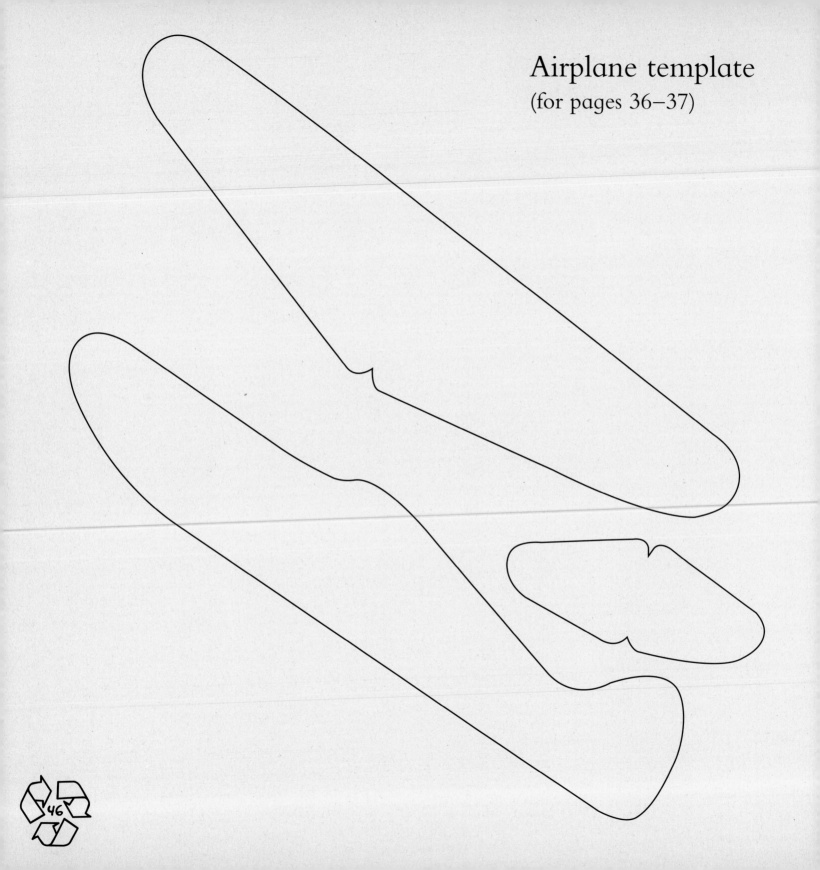

Airplane template
(for pages 36–37)

Leaf template

(for pages 38–39)

Index